A Guide for Using

SOS Titanic

in the Classroom

Based on the novel written by Eve Bunting

This guide written by **Susan Brennan**

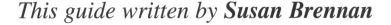

Teacher Created Materials, Inc.
6421 Industry Way
Westminster, CA 92683
www.teachercreated.com
©1999 Teacher Created Materials, Inc.
Made in U.S.A.
ISBN 1-55734-588-8

Edited by
Mary Kaye Taggart

Illustrated by
Wendy Chang

Cover Art by
Dennis Carmichael

Table of Contents

Introduction

There have been countless events that have taken place in history that have been both remarkable and fascinating. We tend to wonder what it was like for the actual people who were involved and lived or died through such occurrences. It is difficult to gain a true understanding of exactly what went on in the various catastrophes that took place over the years. We rely on storytelling and books as aids for gaining understanding. We long to know the facts, but we also want to acquire the details about what really took place in human lives and how those lives were affected.

Through reading, we can interact with the experiences of others and travel to places we never imagined possible. We can also gain insights into people and how they relate to others and the rest of the world. *SOS Titanic* helps us understand the events that led up to the *Titanic's* unexpected sinking and all of the innocent people who perished along with her.

This literature unit will both entertain and provide a wealth of teachable moments. Teachers who use it will find the following features to supplement their own valuable ideas.

- Sample Lesson Plan

- Pre-reading Activities

- A Biographical Sketch of the Author

- A Book Summary

- Vocabulary Lists and Vocabulary Activity Ideas

- Chapters of the book, grouped into sections which include the following:

    —quizzes

    —hands-on projects

    —cooperative learning activities

    —cross-curriculum activities

    —extensions into the reader's own life

- Post-reading Activities

- Book Report Ideas

- Research Ideas

- Culminating Activities

- Three Unit Test Options

- Bibliography of Related Reading

- An Answer Key

We are confident that this unit will be a valuable addition to your literature planning and that as you use these ideas, your students will discover the rich companionship that can be found in good books.

Sample Lesson Plan

Each of the lessons below can take one to several days to complete.

Lesson 1

- Introduce the novel by completing some or all of the pre-reading activities. (page 5)
- Read About the Author with your students. (page 6)
- Introduce the vocabulary list for Section 1. (page 8)
- Discuss the Vocabulary Activity Ideas. Use these ideas to vary the vocabulary study activities that you assign. (page 9)

Lesson 2

- Assign the vocabulary list for Section 1. (page 8)
- Complete one or more vocabulary activities. (page 9)
- Read and discuss the "Author's Note" in *SOS Titanic*.
- Discuss historical fiction and examples of it with the class.
- Define point of view, and have the students skim pages 1 and 2 to determine the point of view from which this story is told.
- Read chapters 1–3, and have the students complete Quiz Time. (page 10)
- Complete Guess Who? (page 11)
- Direct the students to explore related topics with Leaving Home. (page 12)
- Model and assign Mystery Item. (page 13)
- Do Everyday Etiquette. (pages 14 and 15)

Lesson 3

- Assign the vocabulary list for Section 2. (page 8)
- Complete one or more vocabulary activities. (page 9)
- Practice writing dialogue. (pages 19 and 20)
- Read chapters 4–6, and have the students complete Quiz Time. (page 16)
- Complete Teatime on the *Titanic*. (page 17)
- Do the Message in a Bottle activity. (page 18)
- Have the students work on Do the Right Thing, and then discuss their presentations. (page 21)

Lesson 4

- Assign the vocabulary list for Section 3. (page 8)
- Complete Be a Secret Friend. (page 23)
- Read chapters 7–9, and complete Quiz Time. (page 22)
- Do the Fortune Cookie Predictions activity. (page 24)
- Assign *Titanic* Facts and Figures. (page 25)
- Spend some time interpreting dreams. (page 26)

Lesson 5

- Assign the vocabulary list for Section 4. (page 8)
- Complete Better Safe Than Sorry. (page 28)
- Read chapters 10–12 and complete Quiz Time. (page 27)
- Assign Who's Who? (page 29)
- Do Mood Music with the class. (page 30)
- Help the students develop a better understanding of honor. (page 31)

Lesson 6

- Assign the vocabulary list for Section 5. (page 8)
- Read chapters 13–15, and complete Quiz Time. (page 32)
- Participate in a lifeboat simulation. (page 35)
- Assign No-Nonsense News. (page 34)
- Ask the students to each Create a Picture Postcard. (page 33)
- Do a *Titanic* Show and Tell. (page 36)

Lesson 7

- Discuss any questions the students have about the novel.
- Assign a book report and/or research activity. (pages 37 and 38)
- Begin working on one or more of the culminating activities. (pages 39–41)

Lesson 8

- Choose one or more test options to evaluate the students' learning. (pages 42–44)
- Encourage the students to further explore related topics. (page 45)

Before the Book

Before reading *SOS Titanic*, discuss with your students their prior knowledge about the *Titanic*. The following activities will help them focus on the topic and create interest in learning more about this fascinating event in history.

1. Ask the students to study the front and back book covers to make predictions about the novel. Tell them to consider the book title, cover illustrations, and the book description. Record these predictions on a large sheet of chart paper and display them in the room. Have the students periodically refer to this resource during the unit to see if they would like to confirm, reject, or modify their original predictions.

2. Discuss other books written by Eve Bunting. Designate a bulletin board as a "Critics' Corner." Supply the center with index cards that you and the students can use to describe and/or critique other books by this author. Post the completed cards on the board.

3. Define and discuss historical fiction. Ask the students to share the titles of other books that they have read in this genre. Also, ask them what it is about those books that makes them historical fiction.

4. Use a world map to explore the *Titanic*'s route. Ask the class to show the route they think she made, and mark the spot where they think she might have sunk. As you discover additional facts, go back and talk about some of the original guesses to see how close the estimations were.

5. Create a *Titanic* museum. Ask the students to bring in any *Titanic* memorabilia they might have. Allow some time for the students to share their items. Then tell them to describe their items on index cards. Display the items and the cards in an area of the classroom that everyone can visit. (**Note:** You may want to ask the students not to bring in anything too valuable, or if they do, just bring it in for sharing, not to display.)

"OLYMPIC"
45,000 Tons

"TITANIC"
45,000 Tons

TITANIC

The LARGEST STEAMERS in the World

6. Ask the students these anticipatory questions before reading the book:

   • What would you do if you found out you had only one hour of your life left to live?

   • Would you ever be able to leave your entire family to start a new life in a different country?

   • Do you believe that having more money makes someone a better person than someone who has much less money?

   • Is there anyone in your life you would be willing to risk your life for?

About the Author

Eve Bunting was born and raised in Northern Ireland. She was immersed in storytelling from a very young age. She was influenced by people in her culture who went from house to house telling and listening to various Irish folk tales. In 1958, Mrs. Bunting, her husband, and their three children moved to California. She began taking writing courses at a local college and developed a strong love and passion for the art of writing.

Mrs. Bunting has written about many topics, including ghosts, giants, sharks, whales, and other fascinating sea creatures. She has also written about ordinary families, children, older folks, and real problems that people face. She feels as if the possibilities for writing are never-ending. Every day new things happen that can be expressed and celebrated through the beauty of books.

Bunting's first book, *The Two Giants*, was published in 1972. It was about an Irishman by the name of Finn. Since that time, she has written over 150 books that vary from children's picture books to novels for young adult readers. She has also found the time to teach at the University of California in Los Angeles.

Some of Mrs. Bunting's honors include the Golden Kite Award from the Society of Children's Book Writers, the Southern California Council on Literature for Children and Young People Award, the PEN Los Angeles Center Literary Award for Special Achievement in Children's Literature, the Southern California Council on Literature for Children and Young People Excellence in a Series Award, the Edgar, given by the Mystery Writers of America, and recognition by the Commonwealth Club of California.

Some of Eve Bunting's literary works include *Summer Wheels*, *Jumping the Nail*, *Night Tree*, *A Sudden Silence*, *The Sea World Book of Whales*, *Sixth-Grade Sleepover*, *Jane Martin*, *Dog Detective*, *The Sea World Book of Sharks*, *Demetrius and the Golden Goblet*, *Flower Garden*, *Smoky Night*, *Dandelions*, *Sunflowers House*, and *Scary and the Dog Detective*. Her latest books include *I Am the Mummy HEB-NEFERT*, *On Call Back Mountain*, and *SOS Titanic*.

SOS Titanic

by Eve Bunting

(Harcourt Brace and Company, 1996)

(Available in Canada & UK, HBJ; AUS, HBJ Aus.)

On April 10, 1912, Barry O'Neill says good-bye to his beloved grandmother and grandfather. Most people are feeling an enormous sense of excitement about the opportunity to travel on the glorious *Titanic* on her maiden voyage. Barry cannot help feeling sad about leaving the two people he loves most. Mr. Scollins was hired by Barry's grandparents to make sure that he arrives safely in New York. Barry is traveling to America to reunite with his mother and father.

Barry notices that some of the Flynn family will be going to New York on the *Titanic* as well. Jonnie, Frank, and Pegeen Flynn will be traveling in third class (or steerage). Barry hopes that he will not run into them too often in first class, because he knows the Flynn boys might cause him trouble. The boys blame the O'Neill family for their involuntary deportation from Ireland.

Barry spends much of his time wondering what his parents are going to be like. He fondly thinks of his grandparents and constantly admires the wool gloves that his grandfather gave him before he left. One night, while Barry is peering down at a party in steerage, he accidentally drops one of the gloves onto the lower deck. He cautiously creeps down to recover this treasured garment, and suddenly encounters Frank and Jonnie Flynn. Barry is not greeted very kindly by these two rivals; however, this is the night that an interesting friendship is kindled between Barry and Pegeen Flynn. She recovers the glove for him because she is able to understand the importance and sentimental value of such a possession. At this point, Barry starts to realize that class separation is not so important. He begins to see things in a new and different light.

Barry is warned by his first-class cabin steward, Mr. Watley, that he senses a disaster during the crossing. However, he has no idea about the magnitude of the disaster. On the night of April 15, 1912, the *Titanic* does the unimaginable and unexpected. She collides with a large iceberg in the middle of the Atlantic Ocean. The infamous "Unsinkable Ship" begins its fall to an icy death. When the lifeboats are being loaded, Barry makes a quick decision that involves courage, honor, and honesty. He runs off to search for Pegeen and the Flynn boys. In this time of tragedy, petty differences that had existed in the past have no place in Barry's mind. He finds Pegeen and risks his own life to save hers.

In the end, most of Barry O'Neill's friends and acquaintances perish in the disaster. Barry and Pegeen survive by floating on an overturned inflatable lifeboat. They wait, cold and wet, until a neighboring ship rescues them and the rest of the survivors.

Vocabulary Lists

The vocabulary lists below correspond to each sectional grouping of chapters. Activities that reinforce the vocabulary words can be found on page 9 of this book. Because the context often provides clues to a word's meaning, page numbers matching the book version used for this unit have been provided so that the students can locate the words in the book.

Section One (Chapters 1–3)

brocade	18	discreet	18	murmur	17	quay	1
chaotic	21	eminently	22	omen	24	scowls	3
confirm(ation)	29	haughtily	24	ornate	39	seething	1
confrontation	5	lark	20	prestigious	21	veranda	39

Section Two (Chapters 4–6)

brooch	79	forlorn	90	latitude	76	muddle	48
coincidence	48	hovering	79	logo	71	regiment	71
emblem	83	infirmary	69	longitude	76	reluctant	79
embossed	83	kippers	70	mange	71	shilling	73

Section Three (Chapters 7–9)

acute	122	capacity	106	gilded	108	solemnly	105
allay	124	dawdled	110	marvel	131	stern	105
bow	105	elegant	102	nuisance	130	venture	102
canvas	106	fixation	107	pedaling	108	whining	143

Section Four (Chapters 10–12)

davits	177	frail	193	pulleys	177	sedate	174
eerie	157	marrow	154	rudder	191	sleek	158
exasperation	192	precaution	160	seared	181	tiller	191

Section Five (Chapters 13–15)

agape	227	feeble	229	lurched	218	sodden	216
bellow(ing)	199	jaunty	204	magistrate	238	starlings	234
docile	215	keel	233	monotone	197	wallow	236

8

Vocabulary Activity Ideas

This unit contains a vocabulary list for each section. There are many ways for the students to study the words individually, in groups, or as a class. You can help your students learn and retain the vocabulary in *SOS Titanic* by providing them with interesting vocabulary activities. Here are some assignment suggestions.

- Preview a section word list in the following way to check your prior knowledge:

  a. Go through the list and put a "K" (know) before the words that you are sure you can define.

  b. Put a "P" before the words that you think you can pronounce correctly.

  c. Listen as your teacher pronounces each word and gives its definition.

  How well did you predict your understanding of the words?

- Find and copy the sentence in which the word occurs. Underline the word. Then write a synonym or synonymous phrase next to the underlined word.

- Create a vocabulary picture book by writing the words and drawing pictures that illustrate their meanings.

- Sort your word list into categories by parts of speech (noun, verb, adjective, adverb, and other) according to the ways they are used in the story. Write sentences using each word, making sure you are using it as the proper part of speech.

- Write the definitions for the words. Use a dictionary to help you.

- Choose five of the words on your list and see how often you can use them while speaking and writing during the week. Tally your results for the week. What strategies did you use to remember to include these words in your speaking and writing?

- Write a short story, using at least 10 of the vocabulary words. The story may be on any subject you choose.

- Make a crossword or word search puzzle out of the vocabulary words. Trade your puzzle with another student and solve.

- Play Vocabulary Charades by acting out the words.

- Play Vocabulary Concentration by matching vocabulary words with their definitions.

- Write paragraphs which use the vocabulary words to present history lessons that relate to the time period of the book.

- Using at least 10 of the vocabulary words, write a newspaper article about the maiden voyage of the *Titanic*.

- Play Password by dividing the class into two teams. Choose one person from each team to sit facing away from the board. Write a vocabulary word on the board for the other team members to see. Students should alternate giving one-word clues until one of the teammates in the chairs guesses the word. Allow a 30-second time limit for a response. Keep score by awarding 10 points for a correct response on the first clue, nine points on the second clue, etc.

Quiz Time

Directions: Answer the following questions on a separate piece of paper. Write complete sentences.

Chapter 1

1. How is Barry feeling about leaving his grandparents and Ireland?

2. Why do you think Jonnie Flynn asks Barry, "Can ya swim?"

3. Why are Barry and Mr. Scollins seated in front when they board the ship *Pride of Erin*?

4. Why is Mr. Scollins accompanying Barry on the *Titanic*?

5. How did Barry's grandparents find Mr. Scollins?

6. Do you think that Mr. Scollins is suitable for the job? Why or why not?

Chapter 2

7. Describe the stateroom that Barry and Mr. Scollins are sharing.

8. Watley says that the third-class passengers are to stay on the lower decks, and they are notified of this by signs on the gates. Does this information comfort Barry?

9. What is Barry's first impression of the *Titanic*?

10. Describe the treatment of first-class passengers on the *Titanic*.

11. When they are on the deck waiting to depart, what do Howard and his wife talk to Barry and Mr. Scollins about?

12. Why does Howard believe the crash that the *Titanic* narrowly averted when she set sail was a "bad omen"?

Chapter 3

13. How would you describe the atmosphere in the first-class dining room?

14. Why does Mr. Scollins not mention to the other guests at his table that he is being paid to escort Barry to New York?

15. What does Barry do at the dinner table to cheer up Jocelyn?

16. Why does Barry run to return the handkerchief to Jocelyn?

17. What is Barry's plan of action for when Mr. Scollins falls asleep?

18. What do you think will happen if Barry makes his way down to steerage? Why do you think he is so intrigued by the party on the lower decks?

Guess Who?

At this point in the story, you have been introduced to many characters. Some are main characters. A great deal of information has been given about the main characters, and even more will be given as the story continues. Others are supporting characters whose roles are a little more subtle. You are going to select one of the characters to whom you have been introduced. You will need to think about that person and create a prop that represents his or her personality or role in the story. The prop must be handmade, and you should not tell anyone which character you chose. When you are finished, share your prop with the class and explain what it is. Then, allow the class to see if they can guess which character it relates to and why.

Example: Suppose you were to select Barry's grandmother. She often made things for Barry. You might make a sewing basket since you know that she knitted a sweater for Barry. A basket could be made by weaving strips of paper together; its handle could be made from a long strip of construction paper.

Before you choose a character, take a moment to brainstorm several characteristics for each of the names below. This will help you in selecting who you will focus on for your mystery prop.

Barry _____

Mr. Scollins_____

Grandmother _____

Grandpop_____

Mrs. Flynn_____

Jonnie Flynn _____

Frank Flynn_____

Pegeen Flynn_____

Watley _____

Howard _____

Howard's wife_____

Colonel Sapp_____

Mrs. Adair_____

Jocelyn Adair _____

Leaving Home

Even though some of the other passengers boarding the *Titanic* seem happy to be leaving Ireland, Barry already feels homesick. Not only is he leaving his beloved grandparents, he is also departing the country of his youth. He cannot imagine another place being so special.

In order to gain some of Barry's appreciation for his country, each member of your group will become an expert on an element of life in Ireland. Meet as a group to decide who will be responsible for which topic. Find out all of the information you can about your area, and report back to your group. Keep a list of all of the resources that you use. Plan how you will present your findings to your partners. Be creative with your presentation, and think of any props or visual aides that will help make your topic more interesting!

Helpful resources: books, encyclopedias, computers, magazines, travel agents, interviews with people who have visited or lived in Ireland, videos, an atlas

Suggested Topics to Explore

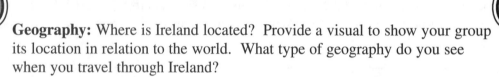

Geography: Where is Ireland located? Provide a visual to show your group its location in relation to the world. What type of geography do you see when you travel through Ireland?

Foods: What types of foods do people in Ireland eat? What are some of the main staples in an Irish diet? Have any American dishes originated in Ireland?

Language: What language is spoken in Ireland? Investigate some of the language that is exclusive to the Irish.

Holidays: What holidays are celebrated in Ireland? How are the Irish customs in celebrating different from American customs? Did any of your customs originate in Ireland?

Education: What is the education system like in Ireland? How is it the same and/or different from what you have known?

Recreation: What do people like to do for recreation in Ireland? What sports, games, and activities do the Irish enjoy?

Resources: What natural resources are abundant in Ireland? What products do they import and export?

Government: By what system of government do the people in Ireland live? Explain how the system works.

Tourism: What are some of the favorite tourist attractions in Ireland?

Mystery Item

Mr. Scollins carries a mysterious bag onto the *Titanic*. He does not reveal to anyone exactly what is in the bag, but he is very protective of it. He locks the intriguing bag into the ship's safe and checks on it every day.

Teacher Directions: Supply each student with an item inside a lunch bag.

Directions: You just received a mystery item, and only you can look inside the bag. Without revealing what it is, write down ten descriptive words or phrases about the item. When you and your classmates have finished, take turns reading the descriptions out loud and guessing each others' mystery items. After the guessing is done, all may reveal their items.

1. _____

2. _____

3. _____

4. _____

5. _____

6. _____

7. _____

8. _____

9. _____

10. _____

Everyday Etiquette

There was an expected form of etiquette, or code of behavior, that was considered appropriate on board the *Titanic*, especially in first class. Watley very delicately informed both Barry and Mr. Scollins that, "No one dresses for dinner the first night out." Watley wanted to make sure that his passengers did not stand out as being people who did not know the correct way to act in certain social situations.

When Barry sat down to dinner each evening, a steward would promptly unfold his white serviette and place it gently onto his lap. Barry knew that when he was seated at dinner, his elbows should not be on the table, and he should politely ask for items to be passed to him.

Listed below are some situations that you might encounter in your everyday lives. The scenarios provided were not handled in the best possible way. Read each synopsis carefully and explain how each situation could have been handled in a more positive way by using proper etiquette. Record your reactions in the spaces provided. When everyone has finished, compare your ideas with the class. (If you need more writing space, use the back of this activity sheet or a separate sheet of paper.)

1. Leslie's parents hosted a surprise 15th birthday party for her. Kim gave Leslie a green sweater, and Leslie said, "I would never wear this because I hate green!"

   _____

   _____

   _____

2. Karen was invited to her friend Danny's house for dinner. Danny asked Karen to pass the potatoes. Karen picked up the bowl, scooped most of the potatoes onto her plate, and then passed the almost empty bowl to Danny.

   _____

   _____

   _____

3. David's mom invited his soccer team over for a barbecue after the last game. She estimated that each person would eat one hamburger and one hot dog. Barry put two hamburgers on his plate, and then he went back for a third before the rest of the team even arrived. He took only two bites out of the third burger and then threw it away.

   _____

   _____

   _____

   _____

   _____

Everyday Etiquette (cont.)

4. Mrs. Brotz, an eighth grade teacher, decided to buy donuts for her language arts class to reward them for all of their hard work. One of the students said, "Why didn't you get any cream-filled donuts? I don't like any of these."

_____

_____

_____

5. Mr. and Mrs. Lawrence sent Melissa a very generous graduation gift in the mail. Melissa never acknowledged the gift, and when she ran into them at the grocery store, she did not say a thing.

_____

_____

_____

6. Erik is having lunch with his parents at a local restaurant. He is just getting over a cold and uses his napkin to blow his nose.

_____

_____

_____

7. Donna was invited to her neighbor's wedding and reception. She responded that she was going, so a dinner was ordered for her. The day of the wedding, she remembered that she had a softball game. She went to the game but did not show up for the wedding.

_____

_____

_____

8. Justin is seated in a restaurant for lunch and notices that his fork is dirty. He begins using his shirt to rub the fork clean.

_____

_____

_____

_____

Quiz Time

Directions: Answer the following questions on a separate piece of paper. Write complete sentences.

Chapter 4

1. Why does Barry have such a difficult time falling asleep?

2. Why does Barry venture down to third class? Do you think that was a wise move?

3. Who broke up the fight between Barry and Jonnie Flynn?

4. How does Barry feel about Watley?

5. What do you think Watley means when he says, "Waves are like people; they don't always do what's expected of them?"

6. Describe the atmosphere in the steerage of the ship. How is it different from first class?

7. Do you think you would have most liked traveling in first, second, or third class as a passenger on the *Titanic*? Explain.

Chapter 5

8. How does Barry explain the gash on his cheek to Mr. Scollins? How would you have explained such a thing?

9. Why does Barry tell Colonel Sapp that a shark bit him on his face?

10. Is Jocelyn's mood any different at lunch on the second day of the voyage?

11. How has Pegeen arranged the 10:00 meeting with Barry, and what do you expect will happen at that meeting?

12. Why is Barry nervous about meeting with Pegeen?

13. What does Barry purchase from the gift shop, and why?

Chapter 6

14. Before Barry leaves to meet Pegeen, what does he do with the glove that he still has? Why?

15. How does Barry prepare for his mysterious meeting with Pegeen?

16. Why does Barry look for a group of at least three people to walk the deck with?

17. How does Barry feel about the time that he spends with the Goldsteins?

18. What does Pegeen have to go through in order to get to Barry in first class?

19. Why do you think Pegeen returned the glove to Barry? Were you surprised by her actions? Why or why not?

20. What do you predict will happen in the next section?

Teatime on the *Titanic*

Regardless of which class passengers were in on the *Titanic*, there was a point in the mid-morning and mid-afternoon when guests stopped what they were doing and enjoyed a cup of tea or hot lemonade and nibbled on freshly baked scones. A scone is a bread-like pastry which has a slightly sweet taste. It is often served with a plump mound of butter and some marmalade or jam. It was customary to converse with other passengers on the ship about various polite topics during teatime.

Directions: Prepare for your "*Titanic* Tea" by researching a topic that would have been of interest in the year 1912. Investigate information about the *Titanic*, political events of the time, popular music or art, roles of women and men, cultural interests, or historical news of the day. Use books, encyclopedias, computers, and *Titanic* materials to help you. Make the scones, tea, and/or lemonade, and be prepared for your polite conversations. Be sure to use your best manners and etiquette.

Scones

Ingredients

- 2 cups (480 mL) of flour
- 2 teaspoons (10 mL) of baking powder
- 1 tablespoon (15 mL) of sugar
- ½ teaspoon (2.5 mL) of salt
- raisins (optional)
- 4 tablespoons (60 mL) of butter
- 2 eggs, well beaten
- ½ cup (120 mL) of cream

Directions

Preheat the oven to 425 degrees Fahrenheit (220° degrees Celsius). Lightly butter a cookie sheet. Mix the flour, baking powder, sugar, and salt in a large bowl. Work in the butter with your fingers or a pastry blender until the mixture resembles coarse meal. Add the eggs and cream, and stir until blended. Turn out the dough onto a lightly floured board and knead for about a minute. Pat or roll the dough about ¾ inch (1.9 cm) thick and cut it into wedges. Place the wedges on the cookie sheet, and bake for about 15 minutes.

Scones are often accompanied with marmalade, butter, and jam.

Message in a Bottle

At this point in *SOS Titanic,* the guests on board the *Titanic* are undoubtedly feeling a variety of emotions. Some are sad to be leaving their homes and heading off to America. Others are excited about the possibility of a fresh, new start. A few are probably even nervous about the fact that this is the *Titanic*'s maiden voyage. Some people have said that she is entirely too big to float in the ocean, and others say that she is surely unsinkable.

Directions: With your teacher's help, break into groups of two to four students. As a group select a character from the book and write a message that he or she might have written. The message should include clues which relate to the character's personality, actions, or attitude about the trip. Once your group's message is complete, slip it into a plastic bottle and secure the cap. Place the bottles from all of the groups in a large container. Each group then selects one that is not its own. Open up the bottles and read the messages out loud. The group which selected the bottle should guess who would have written that message inside.

Example: "I have been reading a fictional book about a ship called the *Titan.* It was a grand, magnificent ship, the most spectacular ever built. Many people thought that she would never sink. On her maiden voyage she was hit by an iceberg, and she sank. All of the passengers perished. I have this strange and uncomfortable feeling about the *Titanic.* I think that something is terribly wrong. Even some of the crew members shared this strange feeling, and they got off before she left port. I would have never stepped onto this boat if my wife had not been so insistent."

(Howard)

Message

_____

_____

_____

_____

_____

_____

_____

Writing Dialogue

One of the most important tasks for the writer of fiction is writing dialogue. In *SOS Titanic* the author uses a great deal of dialogue to express the emotions, actions, and unique qualities of the characters. With dialogue, characters reveal themselves and each other by what they say, how they say it, and what other characters say to them. Writing dialogue sometimes causes problems for a new writer. For dialogue to be believable, it must read as though real people are actually saying the words on the page. If your dialogue sounds artificial or stilted, the reader is not going to take your characters seriously, and you will lose your reader. The following suggestions may help you write dialogue which is believable and appropriate for each character. Keep in mind the ideas below and on the next page as you complete the writing activity at the bottom page 20.

❑ **Be an Observant Listener**

Listen to people speak; close your eyes and imagine people speaking. If you practice doing this, you will soon be able to give your characters words which sound like something a real person would say.

❑ **Visualize Your Characters**

As they speak, picture what your characters look like. Get into the habit of moving people around inside your head and then putting words into their mouths. Write these words on paper.

❑ **Advance the Action**

Move the plot forward with your dialogue. Do not give your characters meaningless things to say. Give them words which somehow carry the story along.

❑ **Vary Your Dialogue**

Dialogue is much more interesting when the wording is varied. For example, you can use the word *said* when you must but don't use it always. Other words that can be substituted for said include *shouted, screamed, whispered*, and *proclaimed.*

❑ **Break Up Your Dialogue**

Sometimes it is helpful to use action in the story to break up the dialogue.

"Go to bed." Mother folded back the sheets. "It's way past your bedtime."

You can also break up the dialogue with emotion.

"I don't want to!" Randy's small face crumpled into tears. "I'm scared!"

Remember that whatever your characters say, the dialogue must always help the story along.

There are certain rules you need to follow when writing dialogue. They are not difficult to learn, but they are sometimes confusing. Use the guidelines below and on page 20 to learn when and how to write dialogue.

When to Write Dialogue

- Use dialogue to help the reader get to know the character.
- Write dialogue for the purpose of telling about what has happened before—for flashbacks.
- Add dialogue to plant clues about what will happen later in the story.
- Make use of dialogue to help move along the action of the story.

Writing Dialogue *(cont.)*

═══ How to Write Dialogue ═══

Enclose the exact words being said with quotation marks, as shown here.

> Jerry said, "I want to go home now."
>
> "I want to go home now," Jerry said, "because it's getting late."
>
> "I want to go home." Jerry stood up. "It's getting late."

In these examples you see Jerry saying basically the same thing but in different ways. The quotation marks enclose the exact words Jerry says. Nothing else.

Words like *Jerry said*, which tell who is speaking, are called *explanatory words.*

Separate the explanatory words from what is being said with a comma or commas, except when a new sentence is beginning.

In the second example above, there are commas after the word *now* and after the explanatory words *Jerry said* because "I want to go home now because it's getting late" is one whole sentence. In the third example above there is a period after *home* because "Jerry" begins a new sentence.

Capitalize the beginnings of new words and new sentences being spoken, as shown here:

> Janey screamed, "The car is going to crash!"

Do not capitalize the second part of a quoted sentence, as shown here:

> "I wish I could go," Tiffany said, "but I have to do my homework."

The word *but* is not capitalized because it is part of the sentence, "I wish I could go, but I have to do my homework."

Writing Activity

Write dialogue for each of the following situations. Use the back of this paper or a separate piece of paper.

- A mother is taking her daughter (or son) out for a special lunch and a movie.
- The football coach and a player discuss strategy for the championship game.
- The school counselor and a student discuss the student's low grades.
- Grandma and Grandpa reminisce about how they first met.

Do the Right Thing

Pegeen sneaks up to the first-class deck in order to return Barry's glove to him. This is a very risky thing for her to do since she knows that third-class passengers are strictly prohibited from crossing class boundaries. She is also well aware of the fact that her brothers would be furious if they found out that she was doing something kind for their enemy. Pegeen returns the glove to Barry because she feels it is the right thing to do. She had seen Grandfather O'Neill give the gloves to Barry the day he left, and she had a feeling that they would mean something special to Barry.

Directions: Break into a small group, and select a scenario listed below. Talk about the situation and determine a resolution with your group. Plan a presentation of the problem and its resolution. Perform your presentation for the class. After the performance, initiate a discussion with the class as to whether or not they feel your group handled the situation in the best possible way.

❏ A new student moved to your district from out of state and started classes today. You notice that his clothes are a little unusual, and he talks with an accent. Some of the kids in your class laugh and snicker as he walks down the hall. He just sat down at the end of your lunch table, and he appears to be alone.

❏ You and a few friends are walking home from school, and you stop at the supermarket to grab something to snack on for the rest of the walk. As you are waiting in line, you notice that the elderly woman in front of you has dropped a wad of money onto the floor. She has not even noticed that it fell out of her purse.

❏ Tony loses his temper because he thinks someone stole his CD that he says was sitting on top of his books. Everyone says that he or she did not touch it, and nobody even saw him come into the room with it. He insists that Eric took it because he knows Eric likes the same group. You overhear Tony say that he will be waiting for Eric after school with a baseball bat.

❏ Your friend Michelle has been looking really sad for the last couple of days. She has not shown up for basketball practice all week. You finally go up to her and ask her what is wrong. Her eyes start filling up with tears. She says she will tell you, but you have to promise not to tell anyone else. You agree. Michelle says that her parents are splitting up and she can't handle it. She has not slept or eaten in days. She says, "I don't care about anything or anyone. My life feels like it's over."

❏ Sheena's worst subject is science. Right now she has a D average, and if she does not pass the next test, she will fail for the marking period. If she fails she will not be able to go on the class trip. You see her cheat during the test.

Quiz Time

Directions: Answer the following questions on a separate piece of paper. Write complete sentences.

Chapter 7

1. What is the reaction of the radio operator when Barry asks about iceberg warnings?

2. Describe the iceberg that Barry and the other passengers see.

3. Why does Watley go over the evacuation procedure with Barry and Mr. Scollins at this point in the voyage?

4. Based on what you have read, how would you describe a caul?

5. Why does Watley ask Barry if his hands were cold throughout the night?

6. Why does Colonel Sapp think that the *Titanic* is traveling so swiftly?

7. How does Watley feel about his ability to see into the future?

8. Do you think it is possible for people to be able to see or know what will happen in the future? Explain.

Chapter 8

9. What is Barry's initial reaction to Watley's disturbing news?

10. Why does Watley tell only Barry about his fear of an upcoming disaster?

11. How does Barry end up with an invitation to join Captain Smith for a tour of the bridge?

12. Why does Barry not write to Pegeen that she should be sure to keep her lifejacket in her room just in case of an emergency?

13. When Barry is on the bridge, he thinks to himself, "I am the monarch of the sea." What do you think he means by that?

14. Mr. Scollins asks a question of Captain Smith when they are on the bridge. It seems to annoy the captain. What is the question about?

15. After hearing Watley's message and visiting the bridge with Captain Smith, does Barry believe that trouble still lies ahead? Explain.

Chapter 9

16. Why does Pegeen not show up for the secret meeting with Barry?

17. When Barry sneaks down to the steerage section, he notices that it is different from first class. What are some of the noticeable differences?

18. How does Pegeen react to the commotion in the hallway and the news about the letter?

19. What do you predict will happen in the next section?

Be a Secret Friend

In chapter seven, Barry decides to secretly send a message to Pegeen's family in Mullinmore, letting them know that everything is all right and that they are having a wonderful trip. He knows that Pegeen does not have the ability to send wireless messages because she is a third-class passenger. He thinks that she might someday realize what he had done, and perhaps she would smile and think about him. This secret gift is Barry's way of repaying Pegeen for returning his treasured glove.

Teacher Directions: Put all of the names of the students in your class in a container. Have students each select one name, and be sure that they do not choose their own. The students will be making gifts for the names that they select. Choose a day that the students can secretly give their gifts to their classmates (put them in their desks, bookbags, pockets, etc.). Have the students guess who sent their secret gifts.

Directions: Create a handmade gift for the person you selected. Fill out the gift card below and attach it to the gift before delivering it. Try to create something that suits the personality of the person you chose.

A Gift from Your Secret Friend

To:

My favorite thing about you is . . . _____

_____

_____

_____

_____

_____

_____

_____

_____

_____

_____

_____

_____

Fortune Cookie Predictions

At the end of chapter seven, Mr. Watley explains to Barry that he has a unique ability to see into the future. He shows Barry the caul that he was born in and explains that people who are born this way have the gift (and curse) of seeing things that others cannot. Mr. Watley says convincingly, "I see disaster."

Teacher Directions: Supply each student with a plastic bag with a cookie inside. (**Note:** Any cookie will do; fortune cookies are not necessary.) Tell the class that they will be making predictions about what will happen to Barry and Pegeen. After they write their predictions on the form below, have them put their predictions into their cookie bags. The "fortune cookies" should then be exchanged, and no one should end up with his or her original cookie and prediction. Allow the students to share the predictions with the class while they are enjoying their cookies. Hold onto the fortunes so that the students can later compare their predictions to the actual story.

Fortune Cookie Predictions

Name _____

My prediction for Barry's fate in the story is . . . _____

_____

_____

_____

I predict this because . . . _____

_____

_____

_____

My prediction about Pegeen's fate in the story is . . . _____

_____

_____

_____

_____

I predict this because . . . _____

_____

_____

_____

_____

Titanic **Facts and Figures**

Directions: Carefully read each word problem below and then answer it in the provided space.

1. The *Titanic* had the strength of 50,000 horses in her engine. If a problem occurred which caused the engine to decrease by $\frac{1}{3}$ in power, how fast would she be capable of traveling in horsepower?

    _____

2. The *Titanic*'s normal speed was 21 knots. If she cut her speed by 20%, how fast would she be traveling in knots?

    _____

3. The *Titanic* consumed 825 tons of coal per day. If a crossing took seven days, what was the minimum amount of coal she would have had to store?

    _____

4. The *Titanic* had 16 standard lifeboats and 4 canvas collapsible boats stored on her decks. If the number of standard boats had been tripled, how many would there have been?

    _____

5. The *Titanic* hit the iceberg at 11:40 P.M. and sank at 2:20 A.M. Express her short lifetime, in decimal form, from the time she had the accident to the time she foundered.

    _____

6. The survivors of that fateful night in April of 1912 totaled 705 out of an approximate 2,200. Express that number as a percent.

    _____

7. The *Titanic* was a majestic 882 feet long. How many inches would that be?

    _____

8. The *Titanic*'s distress call was received by the *Carpathia* at 12:45 A.M. She responded that she would proceed full steam ahead until she reached the drowning ship. The *Carpathia* was 58 miles away and arrived at the scene at 4:00 A.M.

    Round 12:45 A.M. to the nearest hour and give an estimate of how many miles per hour the *Carpathia* traveled to save the victims of the *Titanic*.

    _____

Dream Interpretations

Barry sometimes dreams about his parents. One night he dreams that they are standing by the railing of the *Titanic*, kissing, and when he comes along they pull apart. "Mother! Father!" Barry calls out in his dream voice while running toward them on dream-like feet. But his mother turns her back and looks out to sea, and his father says, "It's only your mother and father, you wouldn't be interested."

Think about Barry's dream. Interpret what you think the dream means in the space below.

_____

_____

_____

_____

Think about a nighttime dream that you have had. Briefly explain the dream in the space below. Then, provide your interpretation of what you think the dream meant. Share your interpretations with the class, if you wish.

_____

_____

_____

_____

_____

_____

_____

Quiz Time

Directions: Answer the following questions on a separate piece of paper. Write complete sentences.

Chapter 10

1. What saves Barry from a second attack by the Flynn boys?

2. Why does Mrs. Adair explain her family troubles to Barry when she talks to him on deck?

3. How do you think Barry feels about Jocelyn's future after talking with Mrs. Adair and her fiancé Malcolm?

4. When Pegeen and Barry first see the iceberg drift past the *Titanic*, what does Pegeen think it is?

5. What are the distant, metal thumps that Barry hears almost immediately after the *Titanic* strikes the iceberg?

Chapter 11

6. How are the passengers and crew members reacting to the iceberg collision at this point?

7. Why does Pegeen become so upset before she dashes off to steerage?

8. Do you think Barry agrees with Pegeen when she says, "They've made me be this way."

9. Reread page 171. Do you think Watley provides any clues that might indicate that there is serious danger ahead and that this may not be just a drill?

10. Barry notices some changes in his stateroom before going up to the top deck for the evacuation. What are they?

11. How does Mr. Scollins handle the news of the evacuation?

Chapter 12

12. What advice does Howard give Barry in the event that the boat sinks and he has to swim?

13. Why does Mrs. Goldstein tell Barry that if he is asked his age by a crew member, he should take off a year or so?

14. How does Mr. Goldstein react to Mrs. Goldstein's advice?

15. Why do the officers call only for women and children to get onto the lifeboats?

16. What makes Barry begin to cry?

17. Do you think that the crew members appear to be organized when they begin loading passengers onto the lifeboats? Explain.

18. Why does Barry not get into a lifeboat when he has the chance?

19. What does the *Titanic* do in an attempt to attract attention and assistance from other ships?

Better Safe Than Sorry

There were certainly enough lifejackets on board the *Titanic* to accommodate all of the passengers and crew. However, lifejackets alone were not enough. In order for the passengers to survive, they needed to be out of the water.

Directions: Put yourself in the position of a White Star Line employee who is in charge of all safety operations on board. You are to plan and design a flotation device that could be used in emergency situations on board the *Titanic*. Investigate what kinds of materials you could use to make such devices. Construct a model of your design and answer the questions below. When you have finished, present the model and its key points to the class. Then test your design's ability to float by putting it into a bucket, sink, or small pool filled with water.

1. What kinds of materials will you need to construct your model?_____

_____

_____

_____

2. Where would you store these flotation devices on the *Titanic*? _____

_____

_____

3. How many people would fit into one of these devices? _____

_____

_____

4. Would your device be used instead of or in addition to lifeboats? Explain. _____

_____

_____

5. What would be the estimated cost for building one of your flotation devices? _____

_____

6. How many of your devices would be needed to save each passenger on the *Titanic*?_____

_____

7. What do you call your invention? _____

_____

Draw a sketch of your model on the back of this page or on another sheet of paper. Then, construct the actual model of your flotation device.

Who's Who?

Teacher Directions: Divide the students into groups and number the groups. Give each group 11 note cards or cut-up squares of notebook paper. Write each of the following quotes on the outside of an envelope. Circulate the envelopes around the room in an organized way. Tell the groups to read and discuss the quotes and then decide who said each one in the *SOS Titanic*. When a group decides who said a quote, they will write the character's name and the group's number on a note card. The card then goes inside the envelope, and the envelope is passed along to the next group. This process is repeated until all the groups have had a chance to discuss all 11 quotes. After every group has seen every quote, share and discuss the answers inside the envelopes. If you would like to turn this into a contest to see which team can guess the most correct characters, keep score on the chalkboard. The answers are listed on page 48.

1. "Together we suffer the colonel's stories of his many adventures."

2. "And you, all starry-eyed over him."

3. "Get him, boys!"

4. "Barry, we haven't met officially. Charity has told me how nice you are to little Jocelyn."

5. "I didn't like that you thought me a monster."

6. "We may have dropped a propeller blade. That's the guess down in the officers' room. If that's the case we'll have to return to Belfast for repairs."

7. "Mr. and Mrs. Jacob Astor are in the reception room. I had the good fortune to have the table next to them, and I caught a word or two of their conversation. Absolutely charming. Lovely people. I hope the table's still free. Probably not, though. There's always some bounder ready to take advantage."

8. "You didn't need to lower yourself to him like that."

9. "What a botheration."

10. "They've made me be this way."

11. "Mr. O'Neill, Mr. Scollins, I am afraid I have some disturbing news."

Mood Music

In the midst of all of the commotion on the deck of the sinking *Titanic*, the ship's band suddenly appeared. All eight of them left the first-class lounge and were led by Bandmaster Hartley. The music that they played supported the party-like feeling that was in the air. Most people were not even nervous at this point. They somehow thought that all of the excitement would be over soon, and they would have an interesting story to tell when they arrived in New York. Did the band know what was going on? Were they just trying to ease the fears of the unknowing passengers?

Directions: If you were the bandmaster on the *Titanic*, what songs would you have chosen to play for your guests on that fateful night? Select one song that you think would have helped to create an uplifting feeling of happiness and comfort, and write about it in the spaces below. Your selection can be something that was appropriate in the year 1912, or it can be a modern selection. Bring the music to class, if possible, and share a sample of it with the class.

Title of Song _____

Name(s) of Artist(s) _____

I think this would be an appropriate song to play because . . .

_____

_____

_____

_____

_____

_____

_____

_____

_____

_____

_____

_____

_____

_____

Badge of Honor

In order for someone to be considered honorable during the 1900s, they would have had to adhere to a set of principles that were considered to be right by most people. Many people made it a real priority in their lives at that time to live by a strict code of honor.

Directions for Part 1: Develop your own definition of honor. Then, skim through chapters 10–12, and find examples of characters you consider to be honorable. Complete the statements below.

My definition of honor is . . .

_____

_____

An *SOS Titanic* character who I think exemplifies honor is _____

because . . . _____

_____

_____

_____

Another character from the *SOS Titanic* who also shows honor is _____

because . . . _____

_____

_____

_____

I did an honorable thing in my own life when I . . .

_____

_____

_____

_____

_____

_____

Directions for Part 2: Make a badge of honor out of ribbon, felt, construction paper, poster board, or any other materials. Write on the badge the name of someone in your school or community who has recently done something honorable. Think about a fellow student, teacher, administrator, parent, coach, etc. Write the action that person did on the badge or on a separate piece of paper (pin this to the badge), and present the badge to the person. An honorable deed is something that is certainly worth honoring!

Quiz Time

Directions: Answer the following questions on a separate piece of paper. Write complete sentences.

Chapter 13

1. Why do the passengers not want to get into the lifeboats even when they see distress flares being launched?

2. What happens that finally sets off a sense of alarm among the passengers on the *Titanic*?

3. How does Colonel Sapp prepare for the ship's sinking? How does this make Barry feel?

4. Where are the third-class passengers, and why are they there?

5. What does Barry do to Watley's caul, and what prompts him to do such a thing?

6. Describe what is going on with Mrs. Cherry Hat.

Chapter 14

7. What suggestion does Mrs. Adair's fiancé, Malcolm, make to Barry?

8. What is Barry's response to Malcolm's suggestion?

9. Why haven't the steerage passengers burst through the gates by the time Barry arrives?

10. What does Barry give Pegeen before she splashes into the water, and why?

11. What happens to Frank Flynn as he tries to slide off the ship?

12. Do Barry's actions while the ship is going down surprise you in any way?

Chapter 15

13. What happens to Frank and Jonnie Flynn?

14. How does Barry end up with a big gash on his head?

15. Why is it so upsetting to Barry that he lost his grandfather's gloves?

16. What does Barry mean when he says, "It will be different in America." . . . "*I can make it different*, he thought, *because I know the way it is and the way it can't be anymore*."

17. What is the name of the rescue ship that saves all of the passengers on the lifeboats?

18. What do you think the future will be like for Barry and Pegeen?

Create a Picture Postcard

Imagine that you were one of the survivors who was saved from the *Titanic*'s tragic fate. The rescue ship, *Carpathia*, came along and brought you to safety. You warmed up, had something to eat and drink, and you were able to get a couple of hours of sleep. Then you realized that you needed to write to friends and family at home and let them know about the tragedy that you and the other passengers and crew just experienced.

Directions: Use an index card, construction paper, or the format below to make your postcard. Plan and design a picture that you think would be appropriate to symbolize the events that occurred. Write a message that includes the details that you consider to be important. (If you are using the postcard outline below, cut it out and draw your picture on the back.)

Survivor's Postcard

Address

No-Nonsense News

Directions: With a partner or in a small group, skim through chapters 13 through 15. Take notes about the details related to the night the *Titanic* sank. Next, plan and produce a videotaped newscast. Decide who will be the newscaster and who will be the survivor (crew member or passenger). Stage the interview on the *Carpathia* soon after the tragedy. Complete the checklist below in preparation for the interview.

Interview Checklist

_____ We completed our research by skimming through chapters 13–15 and by taking notes.

_____ We assigned roles for the newscast.

The characters and the students who will be playing them are . . .

_____

_____

_____ We chose some questions that will be asked during the newscast.

They are . . . _____

_____

_____

_____

_____

_____ We rehearsed the questions and expected answers.

_____ We gathered some props to make the newscast more authentic and interesting.

_____ We planned what we will wear the day we broadcast.

_____ We made arrangements for the video camera and tape.

_____ We scheduled a time with the teacher for recording our newscast.

If there are any additional things to remember, list them on the back of this page.

Lifeboat Simulation

Because there were not enough lifeboat seats for everyone on board the Titanic, only certain people were permitted to board the lifeboats. For those fortunate enough to board the lifeboats, the question of survival still remained. Passengers would have to face the elements, crowded in a small craft, for an undetermined length of time.

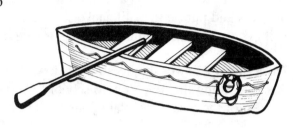

Ask students to imagine what conditions must have been like for these passengers. Some were injured, others had already lost loved ones, and all were wet and frozen. The survivors were now packed into a lifeboat without food or adequate clothing. What was it like to be confined in one of these lifeboats? Although we could not completely revisit this disaster, we can get a sense of what some of the circumstances were like through a simulation. In the classroom follow the directions below to simulate the crowded conditions on a lifeboat. After the simulation, have students write about your experiences and share their thoughts with the class.

Materials

- masking tape
- yardstick or meterstick
- *optional:* rubber raft

Directions

1. Use masking tape and a yardstick or meterstick to outline a rectangle on the floor. Make the measurements approximately 5" x 6" (1.5 m x 1 m). This area will be used to simulate the lifeboat space.

2. Have pairs of students take turns sitting in the lifeboat for at least one hour. They may not move out of that space for the entire time. (Obvious emergencies supersede this rule.) If you are using a rubber raft, the same movement restrictions apply as in the "tape" lifeboat.

Alternative Simulation

1. Push back all the desks and make a masking tape rectangle for each student. The space should be just long enough for the student to sit with his or her legs outstretched and wide enough for the student to sit cross-legged.

2. Direct the students to sit on their rafts for a specified amount of time with no books, no props, no movement out of their spaces.

Write About the Experience

After students have had some time to think about this experience and relate it to the book, ask them to write about the simulation. They should write about how it felt to be so confined and explain some of the things they thought about while they were "adrift at sea." Ask students to consider other physical and emotional factors that could not be presented in this simulation and how the passengers might have dealt with them.

Titanic Show and Tell

Put yourself in the position of a passenger on board the *Titanic*. The ship has just struck an iceberg, and you are told that it is a fatal blow. The captain orders all of the passengers to go down into their quarters and put on their lifejackets. You have approximately five to eight minutes to prepare for your exit off of the ship. Think about the one item you would take with you (besides your lifejacket).

Directions: Answer the questions below. Draw a picture of the item in the box provided. Then, if possible, bring that one item to school for the "*Titanic* Show and Tell." Share your answers below with the rest of the class to explain your choice.

The one item I would take with me onto the lifeboat would be . . .

_____

The reason I would take this item is . . .

_____

_____

_____

_____

Date of "*Titanic* Show and Tell"_____

Book Report Ideas

Display what you have already learned and expand your knowledge on the *Titanic* by choosing one or more of the following activities.

- **Scrapbook**

  Construct a scrapbook that Barry O'Neill might make for himself as a keepsake from his experiences on the *Titanic*. You will need at least five sheets of construction paper and some materials to bind the scrapbook together. Include a journal entry and picture related to each of the following categories: the main character in a scene from the book, a supporting character who was important to the story, the setting of the story, the problem and solution, and how the story ended. Include any additional information of your choice in the scrapbook.

- **Write a New and Improved Ending**

  Put yourself in the role of the author of *SOS Titanic*. You have decided that you do not like the way the book ends and that you want to do things differently. Write a different ending to the story.

- **Newspaper Article**

  You are one of the anxious reporters waiting to break the story and the details of what happened the night the *Titanic* sank. All the world is waiting to hear the news. Write an article that will be on the front cover of the *New York Times*. Be sure to include an appropriate date, headline, picture, and answers to the five W's (Who, What, Where, Why, When).

- **Mobile**

  For this 3-D report, make a hanging display that includes thorough descriptions of these story elements: main character(s), supporting character(s), setting, problem, solution, and theme. Be creative with your design.

- **Filmstrip**

  Prepare a filmstrip and oral presentation. Begin by using pencil to draw the pictures. Then, go back over the pencil marks with permanent markers. Include a title and make sure your pictures are in sequential order. Use index cards to plan your narration of the filmstrip. Present your project to the class.

- **Mural**

  Paint a large picture of a scene from the story. Choose the scene that you consider to be the most important. Write a report on why you thought that event was so significant.

- **Board Game**

  Create a board game using vocabulary, information, and characters from the book. Be sure to include instructions that tell the rules and object of the game. Make game pieces and cards.

Research Ideas

In your reading you were introduced to many fascinating topics such as grand ocean liners, icebergs, class separation, wireless communication, and navigation. Think about what interested you the most and what you would like to learn more about.

Write three questions that you would like to have answered. (Examples: What conditions are needed for icebergs to form? How exactly did wireless communication work in 1912?)

My questions:

1. _____

2. _____

3. _____

Work in groups or alone to research at least one of the questions that you wrote above. You may also choose from one of the topics listed below. Share what you learn with the class. Create a chart, draw diagrams, write a description, or make a speech to present your findings.

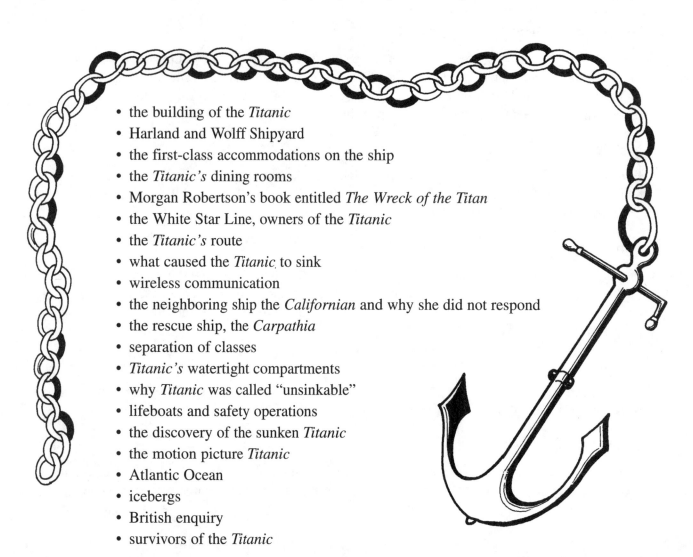

- the building of the *Titanic*
- Harland and Wolff Shipyard
- the first-class accommodations on the ship
- the *Titanic's* dining rooms
- Morgan Robertson's book entitled *The Wreck of the Titan*
- the White Star Line, owners of the *Titanic*
- the *Titanic's* route
- what caused the *Titanic* to sink
- wireless communication
- the neighboring ship the *Californian* and why she did not respond
- the rescue ship, the *Carpathia*
- separation of classes
- *Titanic's* watertight compartments
- why *Titanic* was called "unsinkable"
- lifeboats and safety operations
- the discovery of the sunken *Titanic*
- the motion picture *Titanic*
- Atlantic Ocean
- icebergs
- British enquiry
- survivors of the *Titanic*

Visitors from the *Titanic*

There was such an interesting variety of personalities associated with the *Titanic*. The maiden voyage was a spectacular event that brought together diverse groups of people who had different backgrounds, cultures, education levels, social statuses, and occupations. For years, people have been intrigued by many of these passengers and crew members.

Select a person from the *Titanic*. Plan a first-person presentation for the class. You will talk to the class as if you actually are the person, and you will pretend to be living in the year 1912. Research the person and try to create a costume or prop that would have been appropriate for him or her. The presentations should be approximately two to three minutes in length.

Some *Titanic* Passengers and Crew Members:

- Thomas Andrew—ship's designer and builder
- Major Archibald Butt—passenger
- Colonel J. J. Astor and Mrs. Astor—one of the richest couples in the world at that time
- Molly Brown—passenger who was known for being a very independent woman
- Bruce Ismay—president of the White Star Line; owned the *Titanic*
- Milton Long—passenger
- Mr. and Mrs. Isador Strauss—owners of Macy's department store
- Jack Thayer—*Titanic* survivor
- Ruth Thayer—*Titanic* survivor
- Mr. and Mrs. George Widener—passengers
- Benjamin Guggenheim—passenger
- Harold Bride—wireless operator
- Jack Phillips—wireless operator
- Captain Edward Smith—*Titanic*'s captain
- Ruth Becker—*Titanic* survivor
- Father Thomas Byles—priest traveling on *Titanic*
- Officer Murdoch—*Titanic* officer
- Officer Lightholler—*Titanic* officer
- Captain Rostron—captain of the rescue ship, *Carpathia*

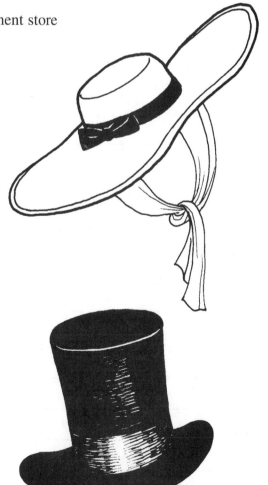

Other *Titanic*-Related People:

(**Note:** If you should choose to role-play one of the following people, choose clothing and/or props that are appropriate for their times.)

- Jean-Louis Michel—led the French expedition to find the sunken *Titanic*
- Robert Ballard—led the American expedition to find the sunken *Titanic*

There are many other excellent choices as well!

Recognizing Heroes

Despite the tragedy of the *Titanic*, there were some people in the fictional *SOS Titanic* and in the actual historical event that clearly stand out as being true heroes. Barry has the opportunity to possibly save himself in one of the lifeboats, but he forfeits that chance when he decides to find Pegeen in steerage. The *Titanic*'s band will go down in history as being brave for playing uplifting music until the very end, in an effort to soothe and comfort the passengers. Captain Rostron of the *Carpathia* is another heroic example. He rushed his ship full speed ahead into the dangerous ice field that destroyed the *Titanic*, in hopes of saving innocent lives.

Directions: Gather several copies of your local newspaper. Read about people in your community who have done heroic acts. Contact one of these heroes or another school or community hero who might have valuable stories to share with your class. Invite the hero to speak to your class. Write a brief explanation of why you consider the person to be a hero in the spaces provided. Then, write several questions that you would ask him or her if you had the opportunity.

My Hero's Name: _____

I think he or she is a hero because _____

_____

_____

_____

_____

_____

_____

_____

_____

_____

_____

_____

Some questions I would ask him or her if I had the opportunity:

1. _____

2. _____

3. _____

4. _____

5. _____

Titanic **Book Talk**

Teacher Directions: Talking about what we read helps us to develop and improve upon our ability to comprehend. Plan a "Book Talk" when the class finishes reading *SOS Titanic*. Emphasize to the students that they need to prepare for the "Book Talk" by planning which points of the book they would like to discuss. Reactions, opinions, likes, dislikes, and commentary about the author's style would be appropriate topics for this activity. Create a casual and comfortable environment for your "Book Talk." Serve light refreshments such as hot chocolate, tea, hot lemonade, and coffee cake. Break the class into groups of five to six students. Provide them with a guideline for their discussions, such as the one below. However, encourage the students to discuss the book in more depth than the guideline. Pass out the guideline prior to the "Book Talk" so that the students may prepare their thoughts on the book ahead of time.

Date of "Book Talk": _____

My overall impression of *SOS Titanic* is _____

_____

_____

_____

_____

_____

_____

The thing I liked the most about the book is _____

_____

_____

The thing I liked the least about the book is _____

_____

_____

I found Eve Bunting's style of writing to be _____

_____

_____

Comments about the characters:_____

_____

_____

_____

Objective Test and Essay

Matching: Match the words with the correct definitions.

_____ 1. quay   a. a thing or happening to foretell a future event

_____ 2. omen   b. a risky undertaking

_____ 3. shilling   c. easy to discipline or submissive

_____ 4. sedate   d. a wharf, usually of concrete or stone

_____ 5. rudder   e. a former British monetary unit and coin

_____ 6. docile   f. parts of a ship used for lowering or raising a small boat

_____ 7. venture   g. calm or composed

_____ 8. davits   h. a broad, flat, movable piece hinged to the rear of a ship

True or False: Write "true" or "false" next to each statement below.

_____ 9. Barry left Ireland because he wanted to start a new life in New York with his mother and father.

_____ 10. Frank and Jonnie Flynn were on the *Titanic* because they needed a vacation.

_____ 11. Mr. Scollins was hired by the O'Neill family to look after Barry on the *Titanic*.

_____ 12. Barry crept down to steerage the first night because he wanted to watch the singing and dancing that was going on.

_____ 13. Jocelyn was unpleasant during dinner because she missed her father.

_____ 14. Captain Smith told Barry and Mr. Scollins that the *Titanic* was fully equipped with lifeboats to meet all of the Board of Trade standards for safety.

_____ 15. Mr. and Mrs. Goldstein suggested Barry tell the officers that he was younger than he really was so that he could board a lifeboat.

Comprehension Questions: On a separate piece of paper, write answers to these questions. Write sentences that show how well you know the story.

16. What does Grandfather give Barry before he leaves, and why is it so important to Barry?

17. Describe the differences between first class and third class on the *Titanic*.

18. How does Barry change the way he views things by the end of the story?

Essay: Respond to one of the following questions on a separate sheet of paper. Provide evidence for your answer.

• Why didn't Barry get into one of the lifeboats when he had the chance?

• What could have been done to prevent the *Titanic* from sinking?

Retelling

Directions: On a separate piece of paper (or recorded onto a tape recorder) retell the story of *SOS Titanic*. You should retell it as if you are telling the story to a friend who has never heard it before. After completing your version of the story, check your work to make sure it includes all of the necessary information. Use the checklist below to assess your own retelling once you are done.

	Yes	**No**	**Comments**
1. I began my retelling with an introduction.	_____	_____	
2. I included information about the main character(s).	_____	_____	
3. I included information about the supporting characters.	_____	_____	
4. I included a description of the major problem or goal in the story.	_____	_____	
5. I included details about how the problem was solved or the goal was met.	_____	_____	
6. I included information about the important events in the story.	_____	_____	
7. I told how the story ended.	_____	_____	
8. I included information about the theme of the story.	_____	_____	

The areas that I need to work on when I retell are . . .

_____

_____

_____

Conversations

Directions: Work in size-appropriate groups to write and perform the conversation that might have occurred in one of the following situations.

1. Barry, Grandmother, and Grandpop are standing on the Queenstown quay, waiting for the departure of the ship. (three people)

2. Barry and Mr. Scollins are discussing Barry's sneaking out of his room and venturing down to the party in steerage where he got into a fight. (two people)

3. A group of first-class passengers go "slumming" in third class just for fun. They meet up with some steerage passengers who immediately know that they do not belong. (four to six people)

4. Barry reunites with his mother and father when he reaches New York. (three people)

5. Mrs. Cherry Hat, her husband Howard, and Captain Edward Smith discuss safety issues of the *Titanic*. (three people)

6. Frank, Jonnie, and Pegeen Flynn discuss the fact the Pegeen sneaked up to the first-class deck to secretly meet Barry and return his glove. (three people)

7. After talking with Watley, Barry bursts out with the message of danger to a group of first-class passengers at the end of Sunday services. (four to seven people)

8. Barry and a group of first-class passengers are standing on the deck when the ship collides with the iceberg. (four to seven people)

9. Officer Harold Bride, a wireless operator, Captain Edward Smith, and another officer, discuss the distress calls that need to be sent out after the *Titanic* strikes the iceberg. (four people)

10. A group of steerage passengers and an officer discuss the situation of the passengers being held in the lower decks until it is their turn to be evacuated. (four to eight people)

11. Officer Murdoch is assisting passengers in boarding the lifeboats. A husband, wife, and their two children try to board one of the *Titanic*'s lifeboats together. (five people)

12. A group of passengers in one of the lifeboats watches as the *Titanic* slips into the icy water, with over one thousand people still aboard. (four to eight people)

13. A group of passengers is in one of the lifeboats, and a man in the water tries desperately to climb in. (four to eight people)

14. Pegeen and Barry are on the rescue ship, the *Carpathia,* after they have been brought to safety. (two people)

15. A group of journalists interviews survivors from the *Titanic* when the rescue ship *Carpathia* pulls into port in New York. (four to eight people)

Bibliography of Related Reading

Fiction

Bolle, Frank and Jim Wallace. *Terror on the Titanic*. (Bantam Books, 1996)

Hamilton, Sue L. *Royal Mail Steamship Titanic*. (Rockbottom Books, 1988)

Martin, Les. *Young Indiana Jones and the Titanic Adventure*. (Random House, 1993)

McGaw, Laurie and Daisy Corning Spedden. *Polar, the Titanic Bear*. (Little Brown and Company, 1994)

Williams, Barbara. *Titanic Crossing*. (Dial Books for Young Readers, 1995)

Nonfiction

Ballard, Robert D. *Exploring the Titanic*. (Scholastic, 1988)

Ballard, Robert D. *Finding the Titanic*. (Scholastic, 1993)

Blos, Joan. *The Heroine of the Titanic*: *A Tale Both True and Otherwise of the Life of Molly Brown*. (Morrow Junior Books, 1991)

Boning, Richard A. *Titanic*. (Dexter and Westbrook, 1974)

Dudman, John. *The Sinking of the Titanic*. (Bookwright Press, 1988)

Kent, Deborah. *The Titanic*. (Children's Press, 1993)

Rawlinson, Jonathan. *Discovering the Titanic*. (Rourke Enterprises, 1988)

Stacey, Thomas. *The Titanic*. (Lucent Books, 1989)

Tanaka, Shelley. *On Board the Titanic: What It Was Like When the Great Liner Sank*. (Hyperion Books for Children, 1996)

Computer Software

Titanic Adventure Out of Time. Cyberflix, 1996. Four Market Square, Knoxville, TN 37902. (423) 546-7846.

Total Titanic: A Night to Remember. Byron Press Multimedia Company, Inc., 1998.

Answer Key

Page 10

1. Barry is feeling unhappy, nervous, and uncomfortable about leaving the people he loves most in the world. His grandparents raised him, and he hardly even knows his parents.
2. It was a threat to Barry. Jonnie wants Barry to know that he is out to get him.
3. First-class passengers were always seated in front of, or before, second- or third-class passengers. That was normal and expected by all.
4. Barry's grandparents hired him to accompany Barry to New York and be his guardian.
5. They put an ad in the local newspaper in Queenstown, Ireland.
6. Answers will vary.
7. The room is large and nicer than those in most hotels, very luxurious. It has a mahogany dresser, four-poster beds with red brocade curtains, a table and chairs, and tasseled lamps.
8. No, he feels that only locked gates could keep the Flynns out. The signs will not be enough of a deterrent for them.
9. He feels that the ship is very grand, elegant, and luxurious.
10. First class was treated much like royalty. Every wish was catered to.
11. They talk about a book entitled *Futility*. In this book a ship called the *Titan* hits an iceberg on her maiden voyage, and all of the passengers perish. Howard has a bad feeling about the *Titanic* as well. Mrs. Cherry Hat laughs at the whole idea.
12. He feels that the avoided crash was a sign or a symbol that something bad is going to happen on the *Titanic*. He is superstitious about these types of things.
13. Answers will vary. They might include formal, festive, elegant, stuffy, prestigious.
14. He wants to give the impression that he is wealthier than he really is. He does not think that his role as Barry's guardian would be impressive to first-class passengers.

15. He puts a blob of cream on his nose and makes a face at her.
16. He knows that it is very important to her.
17. He plans to sneak out and watch the party in steerage.
18. Answers will vary.

Page 16

1. He is feeling homesick.
2. He goes to get his glove. Answers will vary.
3. Captain Edward Smith broke it up.
4. He thinks he is a bit unusual. Watley reminds him of a mechanical fortuneteller.
5. Answers will vary.
6. Steerage is more relaxed, fun, and less stuffy than first class.
7. Answers will vary.
8. He says he fell in the room. Answers will vary.
9. He does not want to tell him about what really happened.
10. Yes, she is in better spirits.
11. She sent him a written message. Answers will vary.
12. He is concerned that it might be a trick and that he might get beaten up again by the Flynn boys.
13. He buys a penknife for protection and a whistle to get people's attention in case he needs help.
14. He puts it under his pillow so that he will not lose it.
15. He puts on his heavy sweater, places his penknife in his pocket, and ties his whistle around his neck.
16. He walks with others for safety purposes. He thinks that the Flynn boys might be intimidated by a group of four.
17. It helps him feel less lonely.
18. She climbs over a gate in steerage and sneaks up to first class.
19. She saw Barry's grandfather give it to him, and she knows how much it must mean to him. Answers will vary.
20. Answers will vary.

Answer Key (cont.)

Page 22

1. He acts as if it is nothing to be concerned about.
2. It is the size of a large boulder. It gleams as smooth as silk, and it is shiny, silvery blue.
3. He senses that something terrible is going to happen.
4. Answers will vary.
5. Barry was wearing his grandfather's gloves.
6. Captain Smith wants to break the record set by the *Olympia* so he can receive a bonus.
7. He feels it is a curse.
8. Answers will vary.
9. He wonders if the disaster is going to happen to him in particular. He worries that the news is related to the Flynns bringing harm to him.
10. He senses that Barry will believe him.
11. He confronts the captain about the icebergs.
12. He would rather see and tell Pegeen in person.
13. Answers will vary.
14. Do the crew members in the crow's nest use binoculars?
15. He is unsure at this point.
16. She never received the message.
17. Answers will vary. Some possible differences are no carpeting, no palm trees, hushed silence, sounds of the engine and the ocean, and the feel of water against the hull.
18. She is angry that the message had been kept from her.
19. Answers will vary.

Page 25

1. 33,333.3 hp
2. 16.8 knots
3. 5,775 tons
4. 48 standard lifeboats
5. 2.66 hours
6. 32%

7. 10,584 inches
8. 19.33 mph

Page 27

1. He blows the whistle to attract attention.
2. She doesn't want Barry to think that she is a monster.
3. He feels that she will be loved and that everything will eventually work out.
4. She thinks it is an old-fashioned ship with a great, white sail.
5. The watertight compartments slam shut.
6. They are not worried.
7. Answers will vary. A possible answer: She was embarrassed that she bowed down to Colonel Sapp, and Barry told her she should not have.
8. Answers will vary.
9. Answers will vary.
10. The bed curtains are hanging at a slight angle, the door on his wardrobe has swung open and is staying that way, his clothes are hanging at a slight angle, and when he latches the door, it swings open.
11. He is very annoyed and calls it a "botheration."
12. Howard tells Barry to swim away from the boat because the suction could pull him under when the boat goes down.
13. He will be able to get a seat on one of the lifeboats and be saved because she does not think they will let him on at age 15.
14. He does not feel that lying about his age would be the honorable thing for Barry to do.
15. Saving the women and children first was common practice at the time, and it was considered the honorable thing to do.
16. He thought of his mother crying if he were not to make it home.

Answer Key *(cont.)*

Page 27 *(cont.)*

17. No. They tried to load passengers into the lifeboats from the promenade deck and forgot about the glass windows.
18. He decides that he needs to find and help Pegeen, and he does not want to look like a coward.
19. The ship fires distress flares at 12:45 A.M.

Page 29

1. Mrs. Adair
2. Mary Kelly
3. Jonnie Flynn
4. Malcolm Bensonhurst, Mrs. Adair's fiancé
5. Mrs. Adair
6. an officer
7. Colonel Sapp
8. Barry
9. Mr. Scollins
10. Pegeen
11. Watley

Page 32

1. They feel it is safer on the *Titanic*, and they do not understand the danger yet.
2. The ship lets out a loud, shrieking sound when one of the *Titanic*'s funnels lets out steam.
3. He puts his full military uniform on and writes a letter to his sister. Answers will vary.
4. They are being held behind locked gates. They are told that they have to remain there until the first and second classes have evacuated.
5. He throws it on the ground because he is angry that third class does not even get a chance to evacuate.
6. She is acting strangely, and she is singing loudly "like a drunk on a street corner."
7. He asks Barry if he wants to try to survive the sinking together.
8. Barry says he cannot because he has something that he needs to do.

9. They know their place and are used to being treated as if they are lower-class citizens.
10. He gives her a whistle so she can blow on it and Barry can find her.
11. His red scarf gets stuck on something, and he cannot move.
12. Answers will vary.
13. They both either drown or are hit on the head with debris.
14. He uses his body to protect Pegeen from a big piece of wood.
15. He feels like he lost a piece of his Grandpop.
16. He means he has learned from what Pegeen has said to him about how people have treated her and her family.
17. *Carpathia* is the ship's name.
18. Answers will vary.

Page 42
Matching/True and False

1. d	6. c	11. true
2. a	7. b	12. true
3. e	8. f	13. true
4. g	9. false	14. true
5. h	10. false	15. false

Comprehension Questions

16. He gives him pair of wool gloves. They are important because they remind Barry of his grandfather.
17. Answers will vary.
18. He begins to see that class separation is not fair. People should not be mistreated because of lack of money, education, social status, etc.

Essay

- Answers will vary. Examples: He wanted to save Pegeen. He wanted to do the honorable thing. He did not want to look like a coward.
- Answers will vary. Examples: additional lifeboats and more cautious speed could have been used. Iceberg warnings could have been taken more seriously.